BUILD
YOUR
Law
Practice
WITH A BOOK

BUILD
YOUR
Law
Practice
WITH A BOOK

21 Secrets to Dramatically Grow Your
Income Credibility and Celebrity-Power as an Author –
Right Where You Live

Kenneth L. Hardison, Esq.
Adam D. Witty

PILMMA PUBLISHING
A PART OF ADVANTAGE MEDIA GROUP

Published by Pilmma Publishing, Charleston, South Carolina.
Member of Advantage Media Group.

Pilmma Publishing is a registered trademark and the Pilmma colophon is a trademark of Advantage Media Group, Inc.
Printed in the United States of America.

ISBN: 978-1-59932-1-851
LCCN: 2010901945

This publication is designed to provide accurate and authoritative information in regard to the subject matter covered. It is sold with the understanding that the publisher is not engaged in rendering legal, accounting, or other professional services. If legal advice or other expert assistance is required, the services of a competent professional person should be sought.

Most Advantage Media Group titles are available at special quantity discounts for bulk purchases for sales promotions, premiums, fundraising, and educational use. Special versions or book excerpts can also be created to fit specific needs.
For more information, please write: Special Markets, Advantage Media Group, P.O. Box 272, Charleston, SC 29402 or call 1.866.775.1696.

Visit us online at **advantagefamily**.com

Dear Lawyer and Prospective Author:

Meeting the challenge of a difficult market is daunting for any profession. Those who practice law face additional problems. You must deal with ethical considerations, and you must present a serious, thoughtful image. Because of the sheer number of legal professionals, it is essential that you stand out from the crowd, that you become the one people think of first when they need legal advice.

We want to encourage you to set aside, for the moment, thoughts about advertising and networking and online "presence." Those are important. But let us take you a little outside the box and ask you a simple question: As a lawyer, are you intrigued by the idea of being a published author?

Think about it. What would it do for you to have your book proudly displayed in your office, in bookstores and online? What would it mean if you were considered an expert in your local area? Can you imagine the increased credibility, marketability and prestige that would flow to you and your practice?

Of course, writing a book is a big project. Is it possible, you wonder, to produce a book without spending hundreds of hours of your time? A book that even your harshest critics will respect? One to which your colleagues and clients (not to mention your mom!) will point to with pride?

We think you'll like our answer.

Yes. In fact, in this increasingly challenging, competitive market, you may decide you can't afford not to have a book with your name on it. And if you wait, you risk seeing your *top competitor* write the book you never got around to doing.

The value of a book for your practice is immense. It's a time-tested way to attract clients. Used properly, a book can build business in a way nothing else can. It gives you a bulletproof marketing advantage, and it can be reused many times, giving you an edge for years and years.

In this short book, we're going to explain to you how you can join the ranks of published legal professionals. We have helped hundreds of lawyers, entrepreneurs and businesspeople get published. And over the years, we have identified the top 21 ways that lawyers can use a book they've written to build their practices.

In the pages ahead, you will learn what the top lawyers, entrepreneurs and CEOs know. And we have included stories of how many successful authors – and not just lawyers – have used their books. It's a way to help you see outside the legal industry's box.

Why is that important to you? Some of the greatest business transformations of all time – even the creation of entirely new industries – were based on borrowed concepts. Henry Ford became, at the time, the wealthiest man on earth by borrowing an idea from a Chicago meatpacking plant. A packaged foods producer changed its entire manufacturing system by copying the pit crews at an Indy race, generating $300 million more in profits in one year. Google leveraged a simple idea and boomed.

May one of the ideas in this book be the spark that changes *your* life.

With Great Enthusiasm & Spirit!

Kenneth L. Hardison, Esq.
President,
PILMMA

Adam D. Witty
Chief Executive Officer,
Advantage Media Group

Why a Lawyer Needs a Book

As a lawyer, you practice locally, where your clients are. Few of them come from a national base, so you have no need to reach out to them with a book, right? That's how the average lawyer thinks.

But do you want to be average, getting average fees, delivering average services, settling for average success, living an average life you don't really enjoy?

A book can profoundly influence you and your practice without becoming a major national best-seller. The success you need first comes from your local area, and that's where you need to focus first on becoming well-known. If you do, you can completely change the nature of your practice to the one you always dreamed about.

Dream big and think big, and your book can lead your professional growth. It can make you a big fish in a pond or, if you want, a bigger fish in a sea. Both ways, you win.

This book will help you see why that is true. We believe you will conclude, "Yes, I need a book of my own." And you need not wait: We can make the work of creating a book as simple as saying, "OK!" You'll hardly need to lift a finger.

Prepare to get excited and learn a thing or two. Let's get started.

Table of Contents

CHAPTER 1

A Book Brings You
Credibility and Celebrity-Power

Robert Kiyosaki, author of *Rich Dad, Poor Dad*, has made a fortune in speaking, coaching, training, and of course his business and real estate interests. But it was Robert's original book that made him famous. It was that book that made him the credible "go-to" expert.

Before Timothy Ferriss wrote *The 4-Hour Workweek*, no one had a clue who he was. The book brought him credibility and fame, and he has since booked numerous speeches with high fees, getting extensive publicity in television, radio and newsprint.

Both authors are now celebrities. They have come to dominate their respective fields as experts. They are considered gurus. What bestowed that status upon them? You got it – a book. A book brings its author the ultimate "street credit." It validates authority.

A recent conference of Inc. 500, representing the 500 fastest-growing private companies in America, had an impressive lineup of keynote speakers. Twenty-seven of the 35 speakers were also published authors. Many of the speakers were chief executives of multibillion-dollar companies.

People put authors on a high pedestal. Writing a book is like running a marathon. Most human beings could never fathom running 26.2 miles and never will. Millions have dreamed of climbing Mount Everest, but only a few have done it. Many dream of writing a book, and if you are the one who has done it, you'll fill that celebrity role.

Writing a book gives you expert status. If you were not an expert, people think, how could you possibly have written a book?

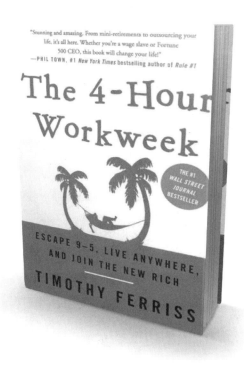

CHAPTER 2
A Book Gets You Free Publicity

Many entrepreneurs daydream about being on Oprah, being profiled in *Inc.* magazine, or being a guest host on CNBC's *Power Lunch*. They at least would like to be featured in their industry trade journals.

For most, it remains a dream. What people don't realize is that the media doesn't care about them, in particular. They care about delivering good content to their readers, viewers or listeners. They want a great story – and a book can be a great story.

Every day, reporters look for people to interview. More than 10,000 people a day are interviewed for radio programs alone. Why aren't they interviewing you? You haven't given them a reason. Sending press releases and hoping for coverage just doesn't cut it anymore. You have to give the news media something to talk about.

A book is something to talk about. Being an author makes you an expert. Reporters want to interview experts for their stories, whether it's for print, radio, TV, or online.

Advantage author Jim Ziegler's main business is consulting to automobile dealers. In October 1998, the year his book came out, Ziegler became a monthly columnist in the industry-revered *Dealer* magazine.

Who do you think reads *Dealer?* That's right, the owners of automobile dealerships – the same people who hire Ziegler. But he was unknown to *Dealer* until he mailed the magazine a review copy of his book. The book ignited the spark that led to his monthly column.

You no doubt will agree that it would be a lot easier for you to attract clients if you were a columnist in your industry's largest trade journal. As Ziegler would be the first to tell you, outside the auto industry, nobody knows who he is. But inside the industry, he's a rock star.

As a lawyer, you could write a local newspaper column and the local media soon would regard you as a valued source and expert to comment on local legal issues. You also could become the resident expert on national legal issues. That well could lead to national publicity and interviews on CNN or FOX News or for articles in *USA Today* or *Newsweek*.

What most lawyers don't know is that media outlets are always looking for experts who can comment and offer insight and guidance. And by authoring a book for the legal profession, you could be among those sought to speak at major legal conferences or to contribute to legal trade journals.

CHAPTER 3
A Book Builds Client Loyalty

Your hot-off-the-press book would be a perfect gift for your best clients – and help you to build their loyalty.

There is a direct correlation between client loyalty and profit, as the world's most successful firms know. They regularly show appreciation to their clients. But most firms do not. Can you think of many gifts of appreciation you have received? Few practices shower their clients with such gifts, but that's what you should do.

You may have heard of the Pareto principle, or the 80/20 rule. It is the rule of the vital few. Made famous by Italian economist Vilfredo Pareto, the rule says that 80 percent of effects come from 20 percent of causes. For example, 80 percent of tax dollars are paid by 20 percent of the taxpayers. Eighty percent of your profits come from 20 percent of your clients. Look around, and you may see that the Pareto principle holds true in many aspects of your life.

What are you doing to thank your best clients? What are you doing to show your appreciation to that top 20 percent who are contributing 80 percent to your bottom line?

Savvy lawyers have a system to continually thank and show appreciation to their best clients. At Advantage Media Group, we classify clients based upon a number of factors. We have elaborate systems and sequences in place for each classification. For example, a Platinum client might receive eight presents and thank-you gifts from us every year. A Gold client might receive six, and so on.

As a gift, your book would double as a client retention tool. A book is like glue that helps clients stick. Not only does it communicate your thoughtfulness, it also delivers a scripted message. What you say and how you say it matters. Your book can be the near-perfect way to get your message across.

CHAPTER 4
A Book Helps You Stand Out

Like us, you may remember visiting Disney World as a kid and riding "It's a Small World." It well may be a small world, but with over six billion people on Earth and more than 300 million in the United States, it's ever more difficult to stand out in a crowd.

But among those six billion world residents are only about three million authors – so if you have a book, that puts you in the top 0.05%. How is that for standing out in the crowd?

Being an author instantly makes you an expert. Being an author instantly catapults you out of the pack. As an author, you are no longer a "me too." Your credibility among clients and competitors soars.

Clients are no longer settling for average service. They have many choices and are looking for competence. The clients you want are those who consider your expert status before they consider your fees. They are comparing you with your competition. What are you doing differently so they will choose you?

Odds are your competitors aren't publishing a book – yet – so with a little effort, you'll find yourself looking back at them over your shoulder while your own practice grows.

In our society, authors are considered experts who can deliver the results that the best clients want. By becoming an author, you will show you have gone the extra mile. You will position yourself to exceed your clients' expectations. You can be known as the authority in your area.

It will pay off for you time and time again. Your clients will refer you new ones over and over again. Taking the time to publish a book might be the tipping point for clients to choose you.

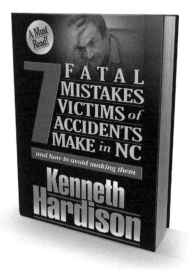

CHAPTER 5
A Book Brings You Quality Referrals

How many of your new clients come from referrals? What percent of your existing clients provide referrals? As a rule of thumb, studies show that roughly 20 percent of your clients will freely give referrals without being asked. Another 20 percent will not give referrals at all. That leaves 60 percent of your clients who probably would refer you business, if you would only ask.

The most profitable businesses report that well over 70 percent of new clients come from referrals. With the cost of advertising and marketing continuing to rise while producing lackluster results, referrals are your best and most cost-effective marketing tool.

In building your practice, you must make it easier for your clients to refer business to you. Smart lawyers provide books to their best clients while asking those same clients to pass the books along to friends, family and business associates who might benefit. The book is an instant conversation starter. It greases the skids, making it easier for clients to give referrals.

A book also allows you to control what clients tell those whom they refer to you. You get assurance that they'll say just what you want. Just because a client does business with you does not guarantee that he or she can deliver your "30 second commercial" in good form. You may have cringed at hearing what even your best clients sometimes say in their referrals. In fact, they may be driving prospects away by saying all the wrong things, unintentionally. Think of your book as a scripted masterpiece – the one your referrals will read.

Give copies of your book to your best clients, and then simply have them pass those books along to anyone who may be a fit for your practice. That helps to ensure you control all your message, leaving nothing to chance.

Pilmma Publishing

(contact) Alison Morse

843.414.5600 ext:103

CHAPTER 6

A Book is the
Ultimate Practice Builder

The cultures of the world have held books in reverence for hundreds of years. They are the oldest and most respected form of communication. They have had an immense influence on civilization, whether printed one at a time on a primitive press or downloaded electronically.

Authors are considered authorities because it is usually an arduous task to write a book; it takes a lot of time, effort, energy and smarts, and, even then, the book might not get published (although at Pilmma Publishing, we do our best to make it easy).

People hold books in higher regard than other communications – such as advertising, which the public often perceives as unreliable. By contrast, they generally think of books as authoritative and therefore are more willing to accept a book's message.

This thinking is imbued in our culture. The reasoning is that a true expert will write a book. By writing one, you immediately benefit from that perception – and you can do it without a lot of heavy lifting.

A book therefore can influence your prospective clients unlike any other form of communication. A book has such power because readers are inclined to quickly accept its message and take it to heart. And even among those who never read your book, you still get a position of authority: You are seen as the expert with the competence they want. We call this the Author's Effect.

The Author's Effect sweeps concerns, objections and hesitations aside. Historically, authors have been regarded as trusted sources of information. Therefore when your clients see that you have written a book, you become such a trusted source. You're the expert they want to retain.

When a client is considering whom to trust with his or her case, a lawyer's authorship of a book provides a powerful incentive. When the buzz is that "he wrote the book," the lawyer is on the top rung of the ladder. And the first to achieve authorship will enjoy that top positioning for years to come. If your competitor has written a book first, you can counter his or her advantage by authoring one yourself. (We can discuss how this is done so that your book becomes preeminent in your area with our proprietary system that is modeled on Apple's success with the iPod.)

CHAPTER 7
A Book Attracts Clients and Generates Leads

Many individuals and businesses use a book to generate leads. Rather than relying on traditional advertisements, they generate the most qualified leads through the power of a book.

Imagine there was a book you could give to all your clients and best prospects that would immediately point them right back to doing business with you. The book you could give them is your book. Consider the following example:

Carl Sewell is chief executive officer of Sewell Automobile Companies in Dallas, Texas. In 1990, Sewell wrote a book titled *Customers for Life*. In the book, he details his company's "Ten Commandments of Customer Service." Any prospect who walks into a Sewell dealership receives a complimentary copy of the book, even if the customer is just looking. Many of those prospects read (or at least skim) the book and learn of the customer service pledges. They conclude that they wouldn't get better service elsewhere and purchase their vehicle from Sewell.

In 1990, Sewell had three dealerships, all in Dallas. Today, he has seventeen, in Dallas, Fort Worth, San Antonio, Grapevine, and Plano. Do you think the book had anything to do with that success?

How can you leverage your book to acquire clients? First, hold a client appreciation party, and provide a complimentary copy of your book as a parting gift.

Second, mail or personally deliver a copy of your book to all your best prospects. Finally, give a copy of your book to every client who enters your doors.

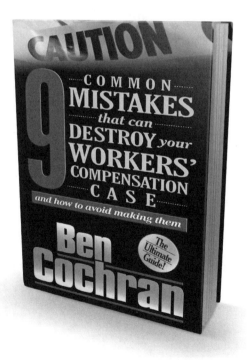

CHAPTER 8
A Book Multiplies Your Message

Too much to do and not enough time – that seems to be our mantra these days. Lawyers, in particular, constantly are pulled in many directions, needing to be in many places at the same time.

A book does allow you to be in multiple places at once – figuratively, that is. It's the power of multiplicity and leverage. The mass media provides leverage. Rather than speaking to people one by one, you can speak to millions at the same time on radio or television. A book lets you to do that, too.

The power of leverage makes the difference between a millionaire and multimillionaire. As the old saying goes, "the first million is always the hardest." But some people make their million and hit a plateau. Others turn that first million into five, ten or twenty million. They do so through leverage.

Leverage is utilizing the strengths of people, processes, media, and economies of scale to do a lot more in much less time. Leverage helps you get the most out of yourself, because you free up your time to work on the activities that are most valuable to you.

Publishing a book allows you to leverage your time by communicating with multiple people at once. While writing the book might require some heavy lifting at first (and we can lighten that load a lot), it will pay dividends for the rest of your career.

Carl Sewell's *Customers for Life* has helped him for over two decades to grow his automobile company from one dealership to seventeen. Same book, and it has worked for more than twenty years. Jim Ziegler, whom we also mentioned earlier, told us that many top executives of the major automobile manufacturers worldwide have a copy of his book on their shelves.

Would it not be quite an advantage if a copy of your book was on the coffee table or bookshelf of all your clients? If you want to take your practice to the next level, you need to work smart, not just hard. Multiply and leverage yourself through the power of a book.

CHAPTER 9

A Book is a Cost-Effective Marketing Tool

A book is the most powerful marketing tool in a lawyer's arsenal, and often it's the most cost-effective.

What is your cost per lead? What is your cost per client? Many lawyers would prefer not knowing, as the answer would reveal a large hole in their marketing budget. Unless you meticulously track and manage your return on marketing investment, you will constantly underperform.

Big "dumb" companies routinely spend $100,000 or more to take out full-page "image" advertisements in national magazines and newspapers. These ads look good but rarely do anything to move the sales needle forward. Big companies can afford to make these mistakes. Small, lean, entrepreneurial organizations cannot, nor can a personal service business like a law practice.

In one package, your book not only is an image advertisement but also a business card, a direct-response ad, and a credibility builder. For less than about $5 per unit, your book can do a lot of heavy lifting – such as helping people to understand what you offer.

A book is a phenomenal tool for explaining the technicalities of the legal services. You sell a technical and complex service. The public has little knowledge of the legal system and how it affects people, and your book will advance the public's appreciation of what you do.

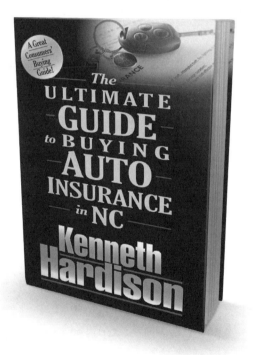

CHAPTER 10

A Book Lets You Be Heard Above the Noise

We are overloaded with information from e-mail, 500 channels of TV, "CrackBerries," blogs, newspapers, radio, billboards and online. To get away from the bombardment, people enjoy peace and quiet in reading – next to the fire or on an airplane, in bed or on the beach. And during that time, a reader will be concentrating solely on what the author has to say.

Lawyers, entrepreneurs and growing businesses find it hard to be heard above the noise. That's why most start-ups fail, if they start up at all. The average American is exposed to over 3,000 unique marketing messages daily, so it might seem nearly impossible for you to get the attention you need.

But close your eyes and picture your best client sitting in his or her den at night reading your book. You control the dialogue, conversation and message. Buying that time would be impossible.

Communication is key. It is the crucial link between vision and execution. Unless you can communicate your vision to your associates, your employees, and most importantly to yourself, your practice will never succeed as it should, no matter how inspired it is.

Effective communication has many components, but the most critical is the message. You must translate your vision into a clear, focused and compelling message that can be conveyed to all. A book is the best medium to do that. You will have the undivided attention of your clients, prospects, and team members. What are you going to say to them?

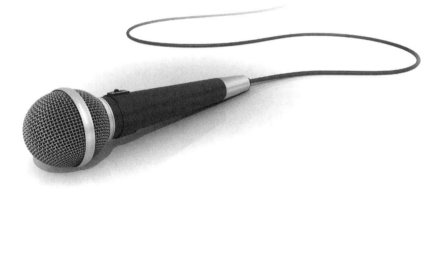

CHAPTER 11

A Book Shares Your Message With the World

T he right book, in the right person's hands, at the right time, can change a life forever. A book can pull someone out of debt, save a marriage, or mend a relationship between parent and child. It could very well change the life of your reader.

People write to communicate ideas and emotions, to challenge and motivate, to reinforce beliefs or deconstruct perceptions. People read for enjoyment, self-enlightenment, education and more. Whatever your message may be, there are people eager to read it.

Many lawyers and other professionals reach a point in their careers when they turn from success to significance. Our altruistic sense drives us to give back, to contribute to the well-being of our fellow man. Many of us have a higher calling and message to share, and we can do so by writing a book, the most powerful educational tool in the world.

Books have enabled people to relate what otherwise might never have been told. Advantage author David Johnson shared his message in his book *Voices of Sudan*.

An amateur photographer, he became a national spokesperson and advocate for the Sudanese people.

There's a book with a message inside everyone. What's yours? Think outside your law practice, too: Do you have a charity, cause or worthy organization that you want to support and publicize?

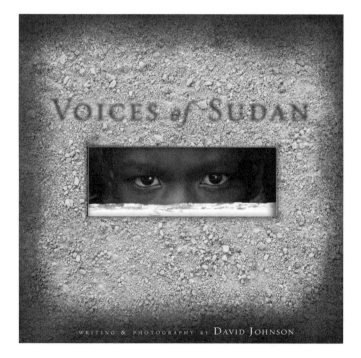

CHAPTER 12

A Book Trains Employees and Builds Their Loyalty

One important way in which smart lawyers use their books is to train and educate staff and build loyalty.

Great practices have well-trained and educated employees – and a culture that emphasizes teamwork. If you invest time, energy and money in training and education, you show your employees that they are an asset of your practice, worthy of such investment. They become loyal team members, and they bring in loyal clients. A practice that works in partnership with its employees significantly improves its service to clients.

However, when you consider how much time you have spent training and educating employees, also think about how much time you have spent hiring replacements for those who left. Think about your hourly rate and how much money you have wasted in training and retraining a revolving door of people.

A book is an extraordinary way to build your team and instill you practice's vision, goals and strategies, rather than reciting them to each employee. And in doing so, you gain their loyalty. A book is like a glue that makes your staff stick with you.

CHAPTER 13

A Book Puts You Above Your Competitors

I f you are in the software business, you probably know that Bill Gates of Microsoft has written a book. If you are in the restaurant business, you probably know that Ray Kroc of McDonalds, Howard Schultz of Starbucks, and dozens of other restaurant entrepreneurs have written books. In fact, many entrepreneurs and CEOs who are at the top of their industry have published books.

Since most lawyers do not author books, you can soar to the top by having one. Not only can a book position you as a "giant," but if the book hits critical mass it can create a dramatic tipping point for your practice.

You can strive for local prominence, or you can go global – and a book can help you do that. When you release your book worldwide, you have the ability to reach out to people around the globe. Your clients may live in your neighborhood or in distant lands. A book solidifies your success locally and extends your authority to broad new areas that you otherwise could not have reached.

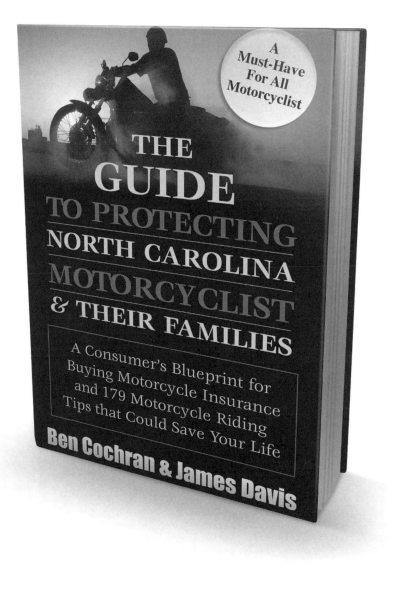

A Must-Have For All Motorcyclist

THE
GUIDE
TO PROTECTING
NORTH CAROLINA
MOTORCYCLIST
& THEIR FAMILIES

A Consumer's Blueprint for Buying Motorcycle Insurance and 179 Motorcycle Riding Tips that Could Save Your Life

Ben Cochran & James Davis

CHAPTER 14
A Book Is a Virtual Sales Force

As a lawyer, you know that there are three ways to grow your business. First, acquire more clients. Second, do more business with the clients you already have. Third, cut your costs of doing business. The first two usually require human energy – namely, employees.

Employees, however, are expensive and have massive needs. When you increase your staff count, you proportionally increase your overhead, headaches and challenges. After all, people are people.

Would you be interested in a proven way to increase your productivity without adding staff? Allow us to introduce you to your virtual persuasion force: your book.

Your book allows you to be in multiple places at the same time, as we discussed earlier. It allows you to have a personal conversation with many people at the same time. When clients or prospects are reading your book, they are focused solely on you – making it far easier to make the sale. Savvy authors will also include direct response techniques, bounce-backs and special offers within their book to keep the phone ringing and the pipeline full of new leads.

A book is a cost-effective, direct response marketing tool that, if used properly, will turn on the spigot of new leads, helping you increase your sales without adding overhead and staff. Best of all, books don't take two-hour lunches, give excuses, or talk back.

CHAPTER 15
A Book Brings You Recognition

Only through a book can you record your thoughts, experiences and history for your family, loved ones, and employees. Have you considered how you will be remembered when your ticker stops ticking?

Will your legacy be how you helped those in your practice? Your community deeds? How will your grandchildren or great grandchildren know you? If you founded your practice, how will team members one day learn about the early years? Your core values are essential to your practice's long-term success. When you are gone, how will newcomers hear about the fundamentals on which you built your practice?

Like a movie or hit song, books can go viral, rapidly gaining followers. They can forever change the world. Take *Chicken Soup for the Soul* or *The Purpose Driven Life* as examples. Both books have made a huge impression for their captivating yet simple messages. If they can do it, so can yours.

We all have a desire to be recognized for our hard work and our contributions. We all want to leave something of us behind. And we all have an ego – and that, too, drives the need for recognition. We express our egos in different ways. Some write a book. It's recognition that lasts.

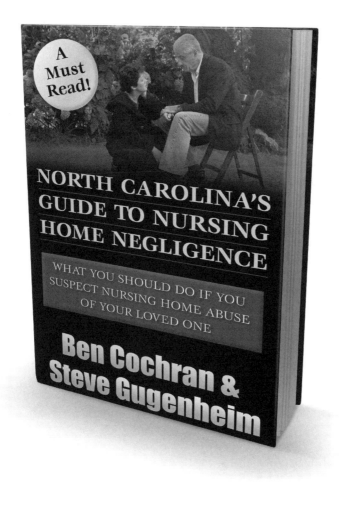

CHAPTER 16

A Book is the Ultimate Networking Tool

N etworking, an essential skill for most professionals, is particularly important for lawyers. It is crucial that lawyers get out into the world and create and maintain relationships.

Henry Ford, according to one account, asserted that if you took away his fortune and left him just a few good contacts, he'd quickly become a multimillionaire all over again. Such is the power of networking – or, as the old saying goes, "It's not what you know, it's who you know."

If you feel you don't have time for networking, that's all the more reason to consider writing a book. Once completed, it will help you network with all the people you want without taking too much time.

A book can do the heavy lifting for you and connect your practice with other people, organizations, and spheres of influence. You can use your book in your advertising media. We offer the books for free on our TV commercials, Web sites, and newsletters. This prompts a prospective client to take action. It's as if the client is holding up a hand and shouting, "I'm a prequalified lead!"

One of our law firms, Hardison & Associates, produced a book called *7 Costly Mistakes that Can Ruin Your Social Security Disability Claim.* We recently handed out the book at a booth at the Cotton Festival in Dunn, North Carolina. A local doctor who also was sponsoring a booth came up to the law firm's display and stared at the book. He was intrigued and asked if he could have some to give to his disabled patients. The response: "Of course!" He was given 250 – and he calls the firm when he needs more.

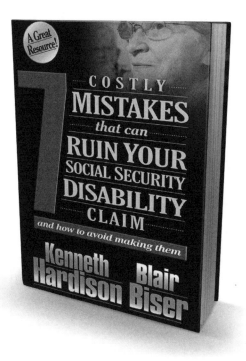

CHAPTER 17

A Book is the Ultimate Business Card

What is the first thing you do when you meet with a prospective client? You slide your business card across the table, right? Start thinking about your book as your business card. Present it to your prospect and say something like this:

"Thank you so much for making time to meet with me. As a token of my appreciation, I would like to give you a copy of my latest book, just published by Pilmma Publishing. I think you will really enjoy it."

As soon as you utter those words and present your book, two big things happen immediately.

First, the prospect will straighten up in his chair and take great interest in everything you have to say. He may have thought of you as a busy lawyer who barely had time for him, but now you have become an esteemed expert who cared enough to give him a copy of your book.

Second, the prospect is now sold on you before you say another word. The reason is simple: Your book has established you as *the* authority on your subject. It's the ultimate sales brochure or letter. Typically, one of your prospect's first questions would have been, "What is your fee?" Now, he's likely to ask, "Would you consider taking me on as a client?"

Because your book is your business card, make sure one of the last pages has all contact information for you and your practice. The contact page is the most important page in an entire 300-page book. Without it, it will be harder to use your book to build your clientele.

CHAPTER 18

A Book Spreads the Word About Your Brand

It is quite possible that you have a cup of Starbucks coffee in your hand as you read this book. In 1999, Howard Schultz, chairman and CEO of Starbucks Coffee Co., wrote a book titled *Pour Your Heart Into It: How Starbucks Built a Company One Cup at a Time.*

Before reading that book, neither of us had stepped foot in a Starbucks store. But as entrepreneurs, we were both interested in reading about people who build thriving companies. After finishing the book, we were so moved by Starbucks' corporate values and the way the company treated its employees, vendors and suppliers that we became regular customers.

Schultz wrote a book to create goodwill for the Starbucks brand and drive new people into the company's stores. It worked. In 1999, Starbucks had 2,500 store locations. In 2008, it had over 17,000.

John Wood is founder of Room to Read, a nonprofit that builds libraries for children in Third World countries. Wood has a fascinating personal story (as most of us do), and he decided to relate that story in a book. The result: Thousands of readers became so excited about his organization that they immediately made financial contributions. Wood's book has brought an infusion of volunteers and contributors to his nonprofit.

Consider what he did as you think about your own prospects. How can you leverage a book to build brand recognition for your practice?

CHAPTER 19
A Book Builds Your List of Prospects

Many years back, Tom Antion, an Advantage author, observed that a personal computer "is an ATM in which you can instantly print money whenever you need it."

Antion's point was that by building a large list of prospects and customers, savvy marketers are able to mail to them at any time and generate instant response, which translates to instant sales. His list of 110,000 customers, prospects and subscribers generates $90,000 to $200,000 per month.

You, too, should be using a book to generate subscribers to your list. You should have numerous references within your book directing them to a free report, article, teleseminar, or something else of value. You want them to say, "*Yes*, I want to hear from you, I want to learn from you, I want you to stay in contact with me."

Another master practitioner of this art is marketing guru and Advantage author Dan Kennedy, known to many as the godfather of direct response marketing and "the millionaire maker." Kennedy subtly weaves free resources – which amount to offers to join his "list" – throughout his book.

Take a page from books such as these, and become an author yourself. Build *your* long list of prospects with a book.

CHAPTER 20
A Book Makes You a Local Celebrity and Speaker

Writers should speak, and speakers should write. A book can do wonders for a speaker, who is likely to get many more gigs and gain status as a local celebrity. Many meeting planners won't hire a speaker who has not earned their seal of approval – a published book. And an author can use speaking gigs to promote a book – and either sell it or give it away.

If you decide to use seminars to promote your practice (which you should do, and we can show you how), your book will be ideal to give to attendees. Whether they read it or not, they will recognize that "you wrote the book" and could well become your clients someday. Some will put the book aside until they have a problem and then use the book to contact you by phone or online. Still others will pass the book along to friends and neighbors. Unlike a brochure, a book doesn't end up in the trash. People keep books.

CHAPTER 21

A Book Can Make You a Client's Only Logical Choice

As a lawyer, you will have a prime opportunity when you write a book to persuade your readers that you are the only logical choice for their legal needs.

Your book should include a checklist such as "Ten Questions You Should Ask Before Hiring a Lawyer." While providing sound advice for each question, you also can highlight what differentiates your firm from your competitors, thereby pointing readers toward doing business with you.

This is an excerpt from one of the Hardison & Associates book:

Here are ten questions you might consider asking a law firm:

> *1. How much experience does your firm have in representing injured people?*

> *2. Have you ever been sued for legal malpractice?*

> *3. Are you covered by a legal malpractice insurance policy?*

4. Have you ever been disciplined by the state bar?

5. Does your firm try lawsuits, or do you refer all of your cases to other firms for trial?

6. Will you copy me with everything you do on my case?

7. What are the qualifications and experiences of the people (both attorneys and non-attorneys) assigned to handle the day-to-day duties of my case at your office?

8. Who at your office (both attorneys and non-attorneys) will be communicating with the insurance company on my case?

9. If I am not happy with your firm the first 30 days after I hire you, can I take my case and owe you no fee?

10. Can you guarantee that your legal fee will not be more than the amount I receive after paying medical bills and case expenses?

If questions such as those are in your book, readers will consider your advice on each one, and you will feel like the obvious choice should a legal need arise. And when those readers come to your practice for an initial meeting, their questions will either consciously or subconsciously be the ones in your book – so you'll be quite prepared.

How We Can Help You Write a Book

Should *you* have a book of your own? We have given you an extensive list of advantages and benefits for a lawyer who writes one. So what's the problem?

You may be thinking that it takes a lot to become an author – a lot of time, money, effort, and frustration. But what if there was a way you could gain all the advantages of being an author without those problems?

The good news: There is a better way, a far better way, that skips all the pain and gives you all the gain. It's our exclusive co-author program from Pilmma Publishing, a part of Advantage Media Group.

What is your goal in having a book? To gain the advantage of prestige, influence, and prospects begging you to be their lawyer, right? To create a marketing advantage that puts you at the top of the hill among your peers, wouldn't you agree?

You don't need to be famous nationwide. You only need to be famous where you live, where your prospects live. We call this being slightly famous. (Sure, you will gain wider fame in your region, and the Internet does help, but your focus will be upon the gains you can make where you live – and where your prospective clients live.)

Traditional publishers present problems that would most likely prevent you from ever getting a book out at all. They outright reject 98 to 99 percent of all the book manuscripts they receive. Without guidance, you would be highly likely to become part of that group of rejects. Who wants a one-in-fifty chance of getting a book published after spending hundreds of hours of valuable time getting it ready?

Traditional publishing has a host of other problems. More than 200,000 books are published every year. The average book run is 5,000 copies. For most authors, after a couple of hundred are sold, the rest gather dust in a garage or storage facility.

Fact: Traditional publishers do a poor job of marketing books, except for already successful authors. They concentrate their marketing and distribution efforts on the top 20 percent of their authors. As a new author, your chances of getting that kind of help are nil.

Other problems with traditional publishing include:

- Loss of creative control: To make it more marketable, a traditional publisher may radically alter the manuscript on which you worked so hard.

- Poor marketing support. The publisher expects you to create your audience.

- For every traditionally published book that does make it through the publishing gauntlet, only one in fifteen succeeds in the marketplace.

That leaves the odds of success at incredibly low levels. Let's do the math:

- 5 percent of submissions are accepted (or 25 out of 1,000; the other 95 percent fail.)

- 7 percent of accepted books succeed once they make it to the marketplace (93% fail).

- .07 x 25 = 1.75, which means:

- Fewer than 2 authors out of 1,000 actually "make it" in traditional publishing.

You have too much to do to play that losing game.

So what about self-publishing? Doesn't that reduce the failure rate? It is, of course, an alternative, but most of us who have tried it won't make that mistake again. Consider these problems with self-publishing:

1. Time. You still have to spend a lot of your time producing the writing. This can amount to hundreds of hours, even thousands of hours. It is not uncommon for writers to take one to two years to produce a book, writing full time. Even after you write the book, there is the time to get it published after you have written the whole thing, typically nine to 24 months.

2. Money. What is your time worth? What is the real cost of producing a book on your own? Even at a mere $100 hourly rate, this alone could total $20,000 to $50,000 in your time just for getting it written – not including the other necessary parts of getting a book self-published.

3. Editing. Even after all that time, effort and energy, you'll need an editor to convert your book into a more readable form. Many authors are finicky about what editors do. It's not fun to see your manuscript, the one to which you sacrificed nights and weekends, gutted by an editor's knife. Moreover there is the back and forth of drafts. It can seem endless.

4. Professionalism. Few self-published works look professional. Remember, the purpose of your book is to establish professionalism, to position yourself as an expert where you live. Book design, covers and layout are crucial. Are you capable of doing it yourself? What would you say to a client who tried to take care of all the details of his or her case?

5. Distribution. A book needs distribution channels. As a self-publisher, you are responsible for these. Do you know how to get your book on Amazon or Barnes & Noble? Who wants to store the books and then, one-by-one, sell them by phone or online? Who has the people available to do that?

6. Frustration. All of these add up and drain your enthusiasm for your "baby" – your book. Getting a book published is a lot of work, time, money, and effort even as a self-publisher. You could labor on your book only to have it fail.

Given all these problems, the conclusion is clear: Both the traditional and self-publishing models are just about impossible for you as a lawyer.

That's why you have an immense opportunity. So few lawyers have books that yours can give you the competitive edge. New clients will choose you, and your existing ones will be more loyal and more likely to refer other cases to you.

And you can do it without the anguish of traditional publishing. Welcome to the Pilmma co-author program.

Pilmma Publishing was established to give you all the advantages without all the pain. Once you are accepted into our authors' group, we make publishing a book easy.

With our unique, hybrid model, you get all the benefits of prestige, positioning, distribution, professionalism, design, and layout of traditional publishing and all the benefits of self-publishing: control, speed, and assured publishing of your book.

You'll find the Pilmma Marketing System valuable not only for your book but for your practice in general. It is designed to bring you fame right where you live – and that's your goal for growing your practice. It eliminates the hassles, frustrations, time, and costs of publishing in the other ways.

It eliminates all the reasons not to be an author.

Here are your next steps:

1. Complete the Pilmma Publishing Questionnaire online. Answer a few quick questions and submit it right away at **http://www.PilmmaPublishing.com**

2. If you want to jump on this immediately, call us at **1-866-775-1696.** We'll chat a bit and see if we are a good match. (Not everyone is accepted. You must be a good fit for Pilmma to accept you.)

Once your Publishing Questionnaire is complete, we'll arrange a complimentary 30-minute call to discuss what's next.

The happy result: You'll have your own book, produced without hassles in record time, with all the glory of being an author and a celebrity – right where you live.

All Our Best,

Kenneth L. Hardison
Publisher
Pilmma Publishing

Adam D. Witty
Chief Executive Officer
Advantage Media Group

About the Authors

Kenneth L. Hardison, Esq.
ken@lawyernc.com

After completing his undergraduate work at Campbell University, where he graduated with honors, Mr. Hardison enrolled in Norman Adrian Wiggins School of Law at Campbell University. Upon receiving his Juris Doctorate in 1982, he quickly went into practice in Dunn, North Carolina.

In 27 years of practice, Mr. Hardison has acquired many accolades, which he attributes to his focused attention to each and every client he represents. He was voted one of the top 100 trial lawyers in North Carolina and is a member of the Million Dollar Advocates Forum.

Mr. Hardison transformed Hardison & Associates, a firm of two lawyers and three staff members, into a 12-lawyer, 42-staff firm in less than seven years by using innovative and cutting-edge marketing strategies. He is a nationally recognized legal marketing expert. He has authored four books, numerous articles, and has spoken at many practice-building seminars for injury and disability lawyers.

He is president and founder of the National Personal Injury Lawyers Marketing and Management Association. PILMMA is the only marketing and management association exclusively for injury and disability lawyers.

Adam D. Witty

awitty@advantageww.com

Adam Witty is chief executive officer of Advantage Media Group, a leading publisher of business, motivation, and self-help books and magazines, with more than 275 clients around the world. Mr. Witty and Team Advantage have redefined and enriched the book and magazine publishing experience for clients.

Mr. Witty is the author of *21 Ways to Build Your Business with a Book* and co-author of *Click: The Ultimate Guide to Internet Marketing for Authors*. His weekly television show, Insights with Experts, can be seen on Internet-television station KaizenTV. In addition, he serves as the publisher of *Author Advantage* magazine and president of the Author Marketing Summit.

Mr. Witty is an in-demand speaker, teacher, and consultant on marketing and business development techniques for entrepreneurs and authors and is a frequent guest on the acclaimed Extreme Entrepreneurship Tour. He has been featured in Investors Business Daily, Young Money Magazine, and on ABC and Fox.

He serves on the board of directors of Advantage Financial Partners, a Peruvian-based micro finance bank; Youth Entrepreneurship South Carolina; and the Charitable Society of Charleston. He is a proud alumnus of Clemson University and happy to call Charleston home.

Special FREE Gift From the Authors

Copy this page and fax to: 919-835-1379

Or visit
www.PILMMA-Gold-Free-Test-Drive.com

FREE
Test Drive of PILMMA's Gold Membership!

1. **2 Months of PILMMA's Marketing Insider's Journal**

2. **2 Months of PILMMA's Exclusive Audio Interviews**

3. **2 Months of Ken's Tip of the Week**

4. **2 Months of Access to PILMMA's Listserv**

5. **2 Months of Member's Only Savings Through PILMMA's Affiliate Programs**

6. **2 Months of PILMMA's Management Newsletter**

There is a one-time charge of $9.95 to cover the postage for ALL 2 months of FREE Gold Membership, and you have no obligation to continue at the Gold Member price of $197.00 per month after your 2 month FREE Trial has ended. In fact, should you continue your membership, you may cancel at any time.

Name_____

Address_____

City/State/Zip_____Email_____

Phone_____Fax_____

Credit Card: **Visa   Mastercard   AMEX**

Card Number_____Exp Date_____

Signature_____Date_____

Providing this information constitutes your permission for PILMMA to contact you regarding related information via above listed means

Tree Neutral™

Advantage Media Group is proud to be a part of the Tree Neutral™ program. Tree Neutral offsets the number of trees consumed in the production and printing of this book by taking proactive steps such as planting trees in direct proportion to the number of trees used to print books. To learn more about Tree Neutral, please visit **www.treeneutral.com**. To learn more about Advantage Media Group's commitment to being a responsible steward of the environment, please visit **www.advantagefamily.com/green**

Build Your Law Practice With a Book is available in bulk quantities at special discounts for corporate, institutional, and educational purposes. To learn more about the special programs Advantage Media Group offers, please visit **www.KaizenUniversity.com** or call 1.866.775.1696.